The Cost
of Freedom

The Cost of Freedom

By Florenda Burns

KASP Publishing Company
Yukon, OK

ISBN 979-8-218-26667-7

LCCN: 2024908907

Acknowledgements
Special Thanks to:

My grandfather, Harold E. Bellmer, who told me his POW experience and showed me the scars on his back for a history report, when I was in 7th grade.

My mother, Beulah Bellmer Boynton, for making copies of all the family pictures and documents, making sure each of her children knew the price paid. We also knew the ENJOYMENT of living and laughing.

My sister-in-law, Library of Congress Archivist Donna Burns: Thank you for all the archival research on my family and Grandpa's WWI Records.

My cousin, Jean Marvitz and her husband Dave. Jean's grandparents are Walt and Elsie Baer. My grandparents are Harold and Erma Bellmer. We enjoyed many visits about the "four friends:" learned, laughed, and love, a great family heritage shared.

Andrea Foster: a true teacher who loves to empower and help her students. Thank you for all the time you invested in me.

My daughter, Susan Burns; without your technical support and encouragement this would not have been completed.

I Thank and Love Each One in this List.

Dedicated to:

All Who Have Served So We Can Live Free

Chapter 1

Morning started early on the Belmar farm, with folks getting up before the sun to milk the cows. Harold did like to have fun, so he often made milk-time into a game with the cats. As he squirted the milk into the bucket the cats would gather around. They became target practice as Harold squirted milk to each one. Sometimes he'd squirt the milk up into the air, and the cats would jump and tumble to catch it. Always most of the milk HAD to go into the bucket. Charles, Harold's father did allow his son to have fun, while making sure milk was not wasted. The cats earned their keep by catching any mouse that came into the barn, so they deserved some milk. Since it was just the two of them, Harold had been helping his father from an early age.

Now it was time to head to school.

Thankfully, their farm was not as far out as

some. Harold ran down the road and across the Crane Creek Bridge. On the other side was the Dunkerton Creamery where they sold their milk. No time to stop now, but he was in town so he could slow down to a fast walk. At the main corner, his friends were waiting. Walt was there as well as Elsie and Erma. The four friends started up the schoolhouse hill. As they climbed the steep hill, Harold told the others he had some news for them: "My father is going to get married."

"To Mabel?" one asked.

"Yes" came the answer. Harold wasn't sure how he felt about this. For so long, it had been just him and his father. Harold's Mother, Sarah, died when Harold was only two years old while they lived in Brunswick, Nebraska. Now being in Dunkerton, Iowa, and the farm built, his father had met Mabel at church and asked her to marry him.

As an almost-teen, Harold was accepting but not quite sure where that left him.

Chapter 2

On April 12, 1902, a wedding was held in the Free Methodist Church of Dunkerton, Iowa. Harold's Father, Charles D. Belmer, married Mabel Clubine, and Harold had a new Mother. Mabel's name changed from Clubine to Belmer, the new spelling of her new husband's last name, and she gained a new family. She had talked to Harold at church a few times, but when his father told him about getting married, Harold was taken by surprise. Now it was official; his father had someone else he cared about. While Harold was glad for his father, he felt a little lonely.

At first, Harold's routine stayed the same, up early to milk the cows, then off to school. An important change to the routine was breakfast. Mabel loved to cook and would have breakfast ready when Harold and his father came in from milking. A couple of days, Harold missed meeting his friends and ran in late for school. Life was changing, but adjustments were quickly made. Harold learned to hurry through breakfast and get to school on time – Mabel's cooking was good, though!

Soon after Mabel joined the family, Charles plowed up an area next to the garden. Mabel had asked him to enlarge it. At breakfast on Saturday, Mabel asked Harold if he would help her plant the new garden. Harold looked to his father- what was he supposed to say? What were Father's plans? Harold didn't know what to say. He had never had a mother before.

Chapter 3

When Harold arrived at the garden with the needed tools, Mabel was already there with the seeds. Harold immediately started working with the rake to break up clots and smooth the soil. The hoe was at the side of the garden for making the rows to put the seeds in.

Mabel called, "Harold, please come here." Harold went to her, wondering if he was in trouble. She had a question for him that surprised him. Harold's father was kind and a good farmer, but as Harold grew up, his father taught him what he knew – farming. His father never asked Harold. He told and showed him what to do and how to do it.

Mabel was ASKING, "Harold, what do you think we should plant? What are your favorites?" Mabel showed him the small sacks of seeds and named them: peas, pole beans, sweet corn, lettuce, spinach, squash… She had a lot! Harold had heard of most of them.

"What are pole beans?" he asked.

Mabel explained that they would need to go into the woods and get some branches or young trees that were straight. They would clean off the leaves and small branches to make them into six-foot-tall poles. The poles would be set up and tied together at the top to make a tee-pee shape, and the beans would be planted at the bottom of each pole. As the beans grew, the plants would wind around and climb the poles.

"Oh, those sound different and fun. I know all the others will be good, but I've never seen pole beans before," Harold said excitedly.

"OK," answered Mabel. "We'll plant the others today, then go find our poles. Let's try to be ready to plant the pole beans Monday or Tuesday after school. How does that sound?"

Mabel was asking him, not just telling him – having a mother might not be so bad!

Chapter 4

Harold found that he liked having a mother. He liked the pole beans they had planted. He liked her teasing his father about smelling like cows and his father answering, "Well, we DO live on a dairy farm." There was laugher in the house, something that had not been there before.

In 1903, Bertha Lou Belmer was born. She was so tiny at first, Harold was afraid he would hurt her with his big hands. As she grew, she began to look around the room for her big brother. She recognized his voice when he came home from school. Harold would scoop her up and spin in a circle, making Bertha Lou laugh.

Mabel would watch them and join in the laughter, thrilled that she had such a wonderful family – living free, able to provide for themselves and others, and to go to the church of their choice.

In 1904, another baby would soon be joining

the family. What would the name be? Harold's parents talked about it while eating supper each night. Mabel noticed that Harold never joined in with a suggestion. Finally, Mabel asked Harold if everything was ok? Was he upset that a new baby was coming?

"No," Harold replied, "but I noticed that everyone has a middle name, and I only have E. What does my E. stand for?"

At first, Mabel looked to Charles, Harold's father. He shrugged his shoulders, not sure what to say.

Mabel asked, "What is your birthdate again?"

"February 4, 1896," Harold answered. "Father is Charles Dage. You are Mabel Jane. Bertha is Bertha Lou. I am just Harold E. What does my E. stand for?"

Father and Mabel looked at each other. Charles slightly shrugged his shoulders, finally saying, "Your mother Sarah chose the initial E. for you." Harold looked a little sad.

Mabel spoke up, "Oh, Harold you have a very special middle name: Back on February 4, 1896, there was an earthquake in Nebraska. That's an unusual word for a name, so your mother, loving you so much, gave you the initial E. for Earthquake. Obviously, she loved to laugh, just like you do!"

Harold was so proud of his middle E. standing for "Earthquake." The next morning, when he met his friends at the corner on the way to school, he told them he finally knew what his E. stood for. They held a game to guess, but Walt, Elsie, and Erma never did. At the end of the week, Harold told them the story of causing an earthquake when he was born. They all laughed, and Harold enjoyed the teasing, because it always ended in laughter.

Roland John Belmer was born a few days later. Their family was growing, which meant activity in and out of the house. As Bertha and Roland grew, Harold loved to chase and catch them up with a good tickling for each one. How Harold loved to tickle and hear the laugher!

Chapter 5

The winter of 1906 was a sad time for Harold and his family. His sister, Bertha, was very sick with a cold. Mabel was thankful for the chickens they had added to the farm. She also was very good at harvesting and drying herbs both that she grew, and they harvested from the woods and surrounding countryside.

Mabel made chicken soup and fed Bertha the warm broth to steam her lungs. She made syrup from honey and dried violets to help soothe her cough. Each day, instead of getting better, Bertha was a little worse.

The doctor was the last resort. There wasn't much cash money on the farm, but Mabel told Charles, "We can give the doctor a chicken. I've tried everything I know. Bertha needs the doctor's help." Charles saddled the horse and went to find the doctor.

Doctor Fisher came in his buggy as he was making his rounds. He checked Bertha's temperature and pulse. He listened to her labored breathing.

Doctor Fisher said, "She has pneumonia. Put a mustard plaster on her chest and keep her very warm. Get as much chicken broth in her as you can and pray."

Charles thanked the doctor, giving him the chicken as he left. Doctor Fisher added the chicken to the others in his buggy. Some he would pass on to people in town that needed them. The rest, he and his wife would eat. With a heavy heart, he went home that night. So much sickness; winters always seemed the worst.

Two days later, Bertha softly sighed, and her soul went to Heaven. She was three years old. There was so much sickness going around that the family prepared her for burial themselves. Charles built her coffin, and Mabel lined it with a scrap of calico.

Mabel washed and dressed her precious little girl for the last time. She wrapped Bertha's favorite blanket around her and placed her body in the coffin. The whole family stood around, weeping quietly as Charles nailed the lid closed.

While Mabel was helping and saying good-bye to Bertha, Harold had been holding Roland. Roland was too young to understand what was going on, but he knew everyone was sad.

Harold started softly singing, "Jesus loves me this I know, for the Bible tells me so…"

By the time he got to the chorus, his parents had joined him, "Yes, Jesus loves me. Yes, Jesus loves me. Yes, Jesus loves me. The Bible tells me so." What a comfort that was not only to one-year-old Roland but also to his father and mother.

Next was preparing the grave. Harold helped his father load the wagon with shovel, pickaxe, and firewood. They went to the top of the schoolhouse hill where the Dunkerton Cemetery was across from the school.

At the cemetery, they found the lot for Bertha, cleared the snow off, and stacked and lit the fire to thaw the ground. After the ground was thawed, they dug the small grave. Sadly, they were not the only ones in the cemetery that day.

While Harold finished the last of the digging, Charles had gone home and loaded the coffin, Mabel, and Roland onto the wagon and brought them to where Harold was. Another friend was there with Harold, Olin Goff, Erma's father. He had been coming daily to help and comfort the families, since their pastor was sick, also.

To have Mr. Goff read Psalm 23 and pray with the family was a great comfort. Then, it was time. Charles and Harold shoveled the dirt in over Bertha's coffin, while Mabel held Roland on the wagon seat and softly wept.

Spring could not come soon enough.

Chapter 6

Spring began to appear: warmer days, snow melting, and mud. On a dairy farm, there is always mud but especially in Spring. As the ground thawed, Harold and his father worked on a new hole between the barnyard fence and the driveway. It was too muddy to get in the fields yet. Often, the ground froze at night. By the time milking was finished, it would have begun to warm up. They were making a big hole. Harold's dad had measured and put markers on the ground, to make sure it was just right. Harold was sad, because this hole reminded him of the last one he and his father had dug.

Charles noticed how silent and sad-looking Harold was, so he said, "Harold, the last hole we dug was a sad one, but this is a happy hole. You like going fishing, don't you?"

"Yes, but eating the catfish we catch is the

best part," Harold replied with a smile.

"Well, this is going to be a catfish hole!" Charles laughed.

Harold did not understand but did not ask any more questions. His father was smart, so Harold knew he could trust that his father knew what they were doing and set to work digging. Finally, they were close to the markers. They worked and made sure the bottom was nice and flat.

"Now, let's go clean up, get Mother and Roland, and go to town. We'll need the flat bed wagon, so if you get ready, first hitch the horses to that one."

Wow. Harold thought, *Father sounds like he has a surprise that he wants us all to enjoy.*

As they came into town, the corner where Harold met his friends for school was the main corner. On the left was the big stone bank that was also the post office. Today, it was closed. On the right was McMillgan's General Store. That's where they were headed on this Saturday. Father stopped at the hitching post in front and got down. Harold had jumped off and going to the side held his arms up for Mabel to hand him Roland.

Father helped Mother down, then said, "Harold, would you take the wagon around to the back? We'll have to load the tank from there."

Harold quickly climbed onto the seat, and his father unhitched the horses, handing Harold the reigns. Harold carefully backed the horses and wagon and headed down the street, turned at the side street and again at the alley. When he got to the end, his father and Mr. McMillgan directed him to get the wagon backed up to the loading dock just right.

Now, Harold saw what the hole had been dug for- a huge water trough! It took all three of them, plus Walt and his father, who happened to be at the store just then. They secured the tank with rope.

Then, Father gave Harold two pennies and told him to get candy for himself and his friend.

After they arrived home, the tank was unloaded by the big hole. The horses were glad to be back in the pasture, and each had a good roll on the grass, still mostly brown but with hints of green. Ahh! Spring was so welcome after the long hard winter they had just had.

Monday, when Harold arrived at the corner, his friends had lots of questions for him. Walt had been telling Elsie and Erma about the huge tank that Harold's father had gotten. They had lots of questions: "Is it a new bathtub? Wow, you could really stretch out in that! Is it for the barnyard? Is your father getting more cows?"

Harold let them keep guessing with a shake of his head no and a grin. Finally, just before entering the school he gave them a hint. Tossing his books to Walt, he put his hands together, palms flat and moved them back and forth. The others were about to ask what that was supposed to mean, when the first bell rang, and they had to rush in.

"Tell you after school!" Harold called with a grin as he rushed to class.

Chapter 7

The catfish tank was very successful. It added another source of food for the family as well as income by selling the extra fish. Harold and his father built a wooden lid to keep leaves and other debris out of the tank. It also kept out the barn cats that liked fish as much as mice.

After school and on weekends, Harold helped his father plant the crops: hay, oats, wheat, and corn. Then, it was time for the garden to be planted but Mabel always insisted that schoolwork came first. Harold was getting older and would graduate from 8th grade in just a few more years. Depending on the weather and how much rain there was most years school let out for the summer before all the planting was done.

Life was busy and full. If Roland managed to come to the barn during milking, Harold would keep his brother near him, so he didn't accidently\

get kicked by a cow. He would let Roland "help" him squirt milk to the cats. Mabel was glad Harold loved his brother so much and was always thankful when they were back in the house safely for breakfast.

One Sunday after church,. Mr. Goff asked Harold and Walt if they would like to come with him for a revival. He had already talked with their parents for permission to ask the boys. Mr. Goff was a farmer by trade. After the crops were planted, he would load a wagon with a simple wooden pulpit, some benches, and a tent. Not everyone lived close enough to a town with a church to attend regular church services. Mr. Goff was a lay minister, as well as a farmer. He would load his wagon and head out into the countryside. His wife Effie, and children Erma, Ruth, Melvin, and Merl would tend to the milking and chicken feeding while he was gone. The two boys were too young at the time to go with their father.

Harold and Walt were glad to go. It would be an adventure and opportunity to see beyond their town.

This time, Mr. Goff set off to the west of town. As they traveled, he would talk to the boys about what they were going to be doing and about God providing for them along the way. Sometimes, the boys would ask him questions, but when it got quiet, he would usually start singing. He would start with songs the boys were used to in church, then branch out into some that were new to them. Many were the English translations of songs older generations had brought with them when they came to America for the freedom to worship God. All along the way, they would wave at farmers and let them know they would be setting up their tent a little farther on. By the middle of the afternoon, they would be looking for a farmer that would let them set up their tent in a field. Often, they would not have to ask but would be invited to use a farmer's field. Having a visiting preacher was an exciting event. The word would go out from farm to farm.

Before the wagon could be unloaded, the right spot had to be found. The field would be cleaned as best as possible, but there would always be signs of animals left behind. The boys would help put down a layer of straw or sawdust, which-ever was available, and then the tent could be set up. The pulpit would be at the front, and one of the benches would be set in the center in front of the pulpit. A quilt would usually be draped across this bench. The other benches would be set in rows for people to sit on.

What a grand time it would be! Ladies would bring food for a meal, either before or after the service. Then, it would be time for church. How the people loved to sing and hear the preaching of God's Word. This was a special time for each community that did not have a church. At the end of the service, there would always be those that, for the first time, realized God loved them and was waiting for them to come to Him. Harold and Walt heard this each Sunday but used this time not only to help others but to talk to God themselves.

For the early teens, this was a special experience to travel beyond their small community and meet new people. Harold realized in a new way how fortunate he was. Life was not always easy, but he was loved, had the opportunity to help provide for his family, and to live where people were free to travel and fellowship together. It would mean even more to him in the future.

Chapter 8

As Harold grew up, time seemed to go faster and faster. There was always so much to do. The farm was thriving and would soon be paid off. The family was growing, with Lee Edward arriving in 1908. By 1910, Harold completed his school training and graduated from 8th Grade. At the age of 14, he was a grown man, able to do a man's work.

After crops were planted, Harold's father would take him to Waterloo, a small but growing city nearby. There, they worked as a team and helped build houses. So now, Harold was getting work training. He already knew how to farm but quickly learned how to build a house. He liked the math involved and the sense of accomplishment when the house was finished.

A year after Harold graduated, Ivan Roy Bellmer was born in 1911. Going beyond his small community made Harold realize how fortunate he was.

Mabel loved to cook and always sent a good lunch with Harold and his father. Sometimes, he and his father shared what they had with other workers. Harold's father could remember when he had hard, lonely years and encouraged Harold to always be ready to help and share with others.

After coming home from Waterloo. the milking had to be done. Then, it was suppertime for two very hungry men and the rest of the family. While Harold was learning what it means to be a MAN with responsibilities, he was also a teenage boy – SO, after supper was Tickle-Time! How Harold loved to hear Roland and baby Lee laugh! Theirs was a hard-working family, full of love and laughter. In the future, the memory of these times would keep Harold going...

Chapter 9

In 1914, when Harold was 18 years old, the Dunkerton *News* began to report trouble over in Europe. The leader of Austria, Archduke Franz Ferdinand was murdered. Within a very short time, the sides had lined up: Austria-Hungary and its allies Germany and Turkey were lined up and ready to fight Russia, Belgium, France, Great Britain, and Serbia. Thankfully, America felt very safe being an ocean away. The newspaper was checked each day. While safe there was still an element of fear.

By September of 1914, French and British soldiers were fighting the German soldiers invading France. While they fought for their countries, in March of 1916, President Wilson threatened to sever diplomatic relations with Germany unless the German Government refrained from attacking unarmed shipping and passenger boats. On May 4,1916, Germany agreed. The oceans seemed safe once again.

On January 31, 1917, the German Ambassador in the United States informed the United States government that Germany would start the next day using unrestricted submarine warfare again. President Wilson went before Congress on February 3, 1917, declaring all ties with Germany had been severed.

During February and March, several United States merchant and passenger ships were torpedoed and sunk. On April 2, 1917, President Wilson asked Congress to declare war on Germany.

While The Dunkerton *News* had been faithful in delivering the news to the people of Dunkerton, Iowa; the war did not affect them in their peaceful world of middle America – that is, until now.

In February of 1917, Harold had to register for the draft into the army. Now, it looked like the draft would be put into use, and an army called up.

U.S., World War I Draft Registration Cards, 1917-1918 for Harold Bellmer

Chapter 10

All Spring and Summer, Harold read the news of the war in Europe. His life went on as normal: up early to milk the cows, then breakfast, and Harold's brothers Roland, Lee, and Ivan were off to school. Harold remembered the days of meeting his friends on the main corner when he went to school. Now, it was time to get to the day's work. He and his father had been helping build some new houses. Dunkerton was growing and houses were being built along new roads running perpendicular to Highway 281. Sometimes, Harold would be sent to the lumberyard in town. There, his friend, Walt, would help him load the boards. Walt and his father both worked at the lumberyard.

On the way home, his father would most days buy a newspaper and stop at the bank to pick up the mail. The Dunkerton *News* was their only way of keeping up with the world events. Since Harold was registered for the army draft, there was a cloud that hung over him and his family: when would he get the notice to go? Would the war end before he was called into service? They hoped and prayed that the war would end soon.

On Sunday, the family would quickly do their farm chores, eat a quick breakfast, and change clothes for church. The four friends from school days would often sit together: Walt, Elsie, Erma, Harold. Each Sunday, as part of the service, there would be a special time of prayer for the Americans fighting in the European War, asking God to intervene, keep the American soldiers safe, and end the war. Many people had family and friends who were already involved in the war, The list grew each week. Harold did not ask to be spared but wondered when he would be going.

In early Spring of 1918, the notice arrived...

Chapter 11

Harold did not have much time. He told the foreman at the house he and his father were helping to build. The news spread through town fast that Harold would be leaving the next day.

There wasn't much to pack as he knew he would be issued uniforms once he got to Camp Cody in New Mexico for basic training. The morning after the notice arrived, Harold and his family were at the Dunkerton Train Depot, waiting for the train. The mail bag was on the hook, but when the station master saw that the train would be stopping, the mail bag was taken off the hook. The station master would hand it to the conductor himself.

Harold's brothers did not go to school that day. They were busy watching over the train trestle that crossed Crane Creek and as far down the line as they could see. A contest was on for who could see the train first. Many of the town's people came to say good-bye.   Mr. and Mrs. Goff and their daughter Erma had come. Mr. Goff asked if he could pray for Harold before the train came. Harold gladly accepted. The crowd was hushed, and Mr. Goff placed his hand on Harold's shoulder.

"Dear God, we ask you to keep your hand of protection on our dear friend and brother, Harold Bellmer.   Keep him safe and bring him home quickly to us. We love you Lord and trust you to be with him."

"The train is coming," yelled Ivan, Harold's youngest brother. Everyone pushed forward giving him a pat on the shoulder then backed a little to give his family time to say a quick good-bye. A last touch to his hand, and it was time to board. Harold waved from the back steps and vanished into the train car as the train moved on. There were other men on the train going to Camp Cody, also.

Harold found a seat and sank into it. It wasn't

until he was sitting when the man next to him asked what he was holding. Harold looked down into his hand, a hankie- Erma's hankie. He could feel the dampness from her tears. Harold tucked it into his pocket and introduced himself.

"I'm Harold," he said extending his hand.

The man next to him shook his hand saying, "I'm James."

As the train rolled along, the men introduced themselves and became acquainted. Some were older than Harold, and some were younger. Stops were made along the way, and each stop picked up more men headed to Camp Cody. That night on the train was long, with many short naps but no real sleep. What a start to army life! It was a small sample of what lay ahead.

Chapter 12

At the train station in New Mexico, trucks were waiting for the new men to arrive. They got off the train and onto the trucks. As soon as a truck was full, it left for the military base. There, the men were ordered off. No one spoke they YELLED! The men were lined up in rows, and officers went down the rows gathering names. Then, they took the oath, fragment by fragment, full volume. Harold's throat was dry by the time it was over but that didn't matter. Here, you took orders and did not complain or ask for favors. He loved America and had enjoyed a life of living and working on the farm. Harold was glad to serve his country but was scared of what was coming at the same time.

After the oath, the men were marched to a building where they each had a turn at having all their hair shaved off. Next came the shots, several in each arm. After that they finally were given a stack of uniforms and other essentials before being lead to the barracks. They were told to change and be ready in 15 minutes. There was no time to think or fuss. Each soldier threw his things on a bed and quickly put on his first uniform. They rushed out the door to line up in front of his barracks where the captain was waiting. Roll call was taken as quickly as possible, and they became a unit on the march. Part of the time, they had to "double-time" it, an almost run. By dark, they were exhausted, quickly ate their rations and dropped into bed. After the night on the train, sleep came quickly and easily.

For five months, Harold learned not only the basics of taking orders, marching, running, and creeping (or the belly crawl,) but he also learned to take care of his weapon and how to use it. Harold had an advantage over, some of the men for he and his father had often hunted for meat for the family.

This was different, though. Often, the target would be in the shape of a person. They learned about crippling shots and deadly shots. They also learned basic first aid, but that would only be used after the battle stopped. There was a lot about basic training that was hard to think about. Harold, James, and another man, Fred, became good friends during this time. They hoped they would be able to stay together when they shipped out.

Chapter 13

Finally, the word came in late June to pack up their duffel bags. Their unit was getting ready to ship out. First was the long train trip to Boston. The train was full but not PACKED. Everyone had a seat, with no one sitting on the floor like when they went to Camp Cody.

New Mexico was very different than Iowa, with its dried landscape and adobe houses. On the way to Boston, the landscape out the windows was changing. It was greener. Parts were forested, and they passed through many towns. The three friends, Harold, James, and Fred were thankful to be going together. One of the special bonds they had as friends was Jesus Christ. They shared with each other the times when they had trusted Jesus to be their Savior. Harold told James and Fred about helping Mr. Goff with the summer tent revivals.

Boston was huge, compared to anything the

three men had seen, but there was no time to explore. Again, it was off the train and onto trucks. The men were taken directly to the seaport. The officers were barking orders to their units. Harold and his friends had to be careful to keep up and NOT get mixed up with other units. There were several ships being loaded.

On June 30, 1918, Private Harold E. Bellmer set sail with his Infantry Unit on the *Runic*, United States Army Transport Ship.

U.S., WWI Troop Transport Ships, 1918-1919

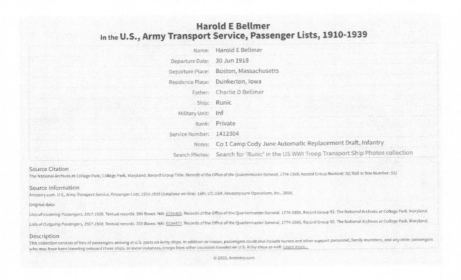

Harold E Bellmer
in the **U.S., Army Transport Service, Passenger Lists, 1910-1939**

Name:	Harold E Bellmer
Departure Date:	30 Jun 1918
Departure Place:	Boston, Massachusetts
Residence Place:	Dunkerton, Iowa
Father:	Charlie D Bellmer
Ship:	Runic
Military Unit:	Inf
Rank:	Private
Service Number:	1412304
Notes:	Co 1 Camp Cody June Automatic Replacement Draft, Infantry
Search Photos:	Search for 'Runic' in the US WWI Troop Transport Ship Photos collection

Source Citation
The National Archives at College Park; College Park, Maryland; Record Group Title: *Records of the Office of the Quartermaster General, 1774-1985*; Record Group Number: 92; Roll or Box Number: 552

Source Information
Ancestry.com. *U.S., Army Transport Service, Passenger Lists, 1910-1939* [database on-line]. Lehi, UT, USA: Ancestry.com Operations, Inc., 2016.

Original data:
Lists of Incoming Passengers, 1917-1938. Textual records. 360 Boxes. NAI: 6234465. Records of the Office of the Quartermaster General, 1774-1985, Record Group 92. The National Archives at College Park, Maryland.
Lists of Outgoing Passengers, 1917-1938. Textual records. 255 Boxes. NAI: 6234477. Records of the Office of the Quartermaster General, 1774-1985, Record Group 92. The National Archives at College Park, Maryland.

Description
This collection consists of lists of passengers arriving at U.S. ports on Army ships. In addition to troops, passengers could also include nurses and other support personnel, family members, and any other passengers who may have been traveling onboard these ships. In some instances, troops from other countries traveled on U.S. Army ships as well. Learn more...

© 2020, Ancestry.com

Sea travel was a new experience as the ship was not just going forward but also up and down. Some of the men became very seasick. Those that were not violently ill were put through drills each day. The men needed to be fit and ready to fight as soon as the Atlantic Ocean was crossed. Finally, land was sighted, and they pulled into the French port. Quickly unloaded, they were transported to their assigned camp. No barracks here; tents were the best they had…

Chapter 14

In France, the army was on the move. Before long, Regiment 59 Infantry 4 Division was called to go. They were loaded onto the narrow gage train: box cars only, 40 men to a car, standing room only. This was not America; immediately, they were IN the war. This is what they had been training for, but no amount of training could prepare them for the reality. As often as possible, James, Harold, and Fred would try to position themselves so they would be near each other. They worked well together, each fighting while also being aware of their friends. They could help keep each other safe while covering a larger area in front of them. Soon, Harold and his friends were at the front line of the fighting.

They were in a huge forest. Harold had not seen such big tree trunks, both an advantage and disadvantage. The trunks were big enough to hide behind, but the German soldiers could hide behind them, also. The ground was covered with the leaves of many Falls. They made a thick carpet and surprisingly were soft, not crisp and crunchy like back Home. The dampness of the forest probably had a lot to do with the stillness, but even the damp leaves could not hide the gunfire and sounds of war.

Men around them were being shot. There was a German sniper on a rise of ground that gave him the ability to see the Americans between the ground and the forest foliage. Their commander saw how the three friends were working together and worked his way to them. He commanded them to work their way forward and take out the sniper. A quick nod told the commander that they heard and understood.

In only a few seconds, the three men saw their path, and as one, their plan was in action. Harold and Fred kept up a fast volley of fire while

James moved forward. Then, James and Fred from two different positions fired while Harold ran forward. Next, James and Harold held off the Germans so Fred could run forward. The Germans, while seeing what was happening, took many casualties as Harold, James, and Fred were moving forward. The American firing was getting less and less, telling the friends that MANY in their unit had been shot and killed.

James was the first of the friends to be hit. As Harold made his next run forward, he grabbed James and dragged him to safety behind a fallen log. Now, it was Fred's turn to advance. Harold kept a volley of shots going, while noticing there was almost silence from the soldiers around him. Fred continued to the log but had a bad wound by the time he got there.

There was no way forward now, and the forest was growing quiet. Harold grabbed leaves and covered his friends and himself as best he could.

The three men lay still as the forest became quiet. The wait seemed like an eternity to Harold. He felt first James, then Fred, become still...cold...

The Germans were slowly moving through the forest. They were checking all American soldiers that were still in the forest. A few had retreated and escaped back to French safety. Harold lay listening. He felt Fred's body move against him as a German soldier checked him. Then the rifle barrel was thrust into Harold's side. He was lying face-down and tried to react as he had felt Fred react. Then, he felt James being checked. Harold did not dare move. All those games of hide and seek with his younger brothers were paying off. He had fooled the Germans. Now, if they would just leave the forest, he could escape back to the French encampment where his unit was stationed.

Chapter 15

Harold could hear footsteps around where he and his two friends lay in the leaves. He could tell they were German soldiers because he could not understand what they were saying. Suddenly, a hand grabbed his shirt and jerked him up. He stumbled forward as he was pushed by the barrel end of a rifle. The German soldiers were gathering up the American soldiers that were still alive. Harold had fooled the first soldier that checked him, but somehow another soldier realized he was alive even though his friends were not. All the Americans were herded in front of the German soldiers.

Harold had a fleeting thought: *I wonder if this is how the cows feel back home.* The thought of home made him sad and determined at the same time. As his stumbled along, he DETERMINED he would not let the Germans win.

He would do right, AND he would LIVE! It was July 16, 1918.

On August 11, 1918, Charles Bellmer, Harold's father, received an Army telegram saying that Private Harold Bellmer was listed as Missing in Action. Harold's family did three things: cried, prayed, and told their friend Olin Goff. Olin immediately told his daughter, Erma, to go tell the neighbor; thus starting the Dunkerton town prayer chain.

Back in Germany, Harold would only give his name, rank, and serial number as they had been taught in boot camp: "Harold E. Bellmer, Private, First Class, 1412304." The German officer that spoke English and questioned Harold and the other prisoners would often ask Harold to spell his last name.

"B E L L M E R," Harold would spell proudly; he was American after all. The officer enjoyed slapping and hitting the prisoners. Harold received many bruises but stayed determined not to let the Germans win.

After a day of questions and standing at attention in the hot sun while the others were being questioned, the prisoners were each given a bowl of potato water soup, if you could call it soup. It was the cooking water from the potatoes the Germans ate. There was nothing of substance in it, but at least, it was wet and quenched their thirst a bit. This was the routine for several days. Then, the Germans decided to step up their tactics...

Chapter 16

Early in the morning. the prisoners were marched to another camp. It was getting dark, and there had been nothing to eat all day. The prisoners were led to a building, and at the door, each was given a bowl. This bowl did not contain potato water; it was the water the roots of shrubs had been boiled in. Many of the prisoners were sick that night, but Harold was DETERMINED and knew he had to keep it down to live.

The next morning, Harold and the other prisoners were marched to a field. Harold thought they might be put to work, but the sight before them made them wonder what was in the field. They had never seen anything like it. The sight before them looked like huge metal clamshells, all in rows. The smell was awful! The prisoners were ordered to halt and to remove their shirts. Then, as they were marched down the rows, each prisoner was forced to step into a shell. All too soon, Harold was being pushed into the clamshell, and as the lid was quickly pushed down on him, it forced him into a crouched-ball position. The inside of the lid was covered with rows of triangular spikes that dug into his back. As the sun continued to rise, the lid became a hot piece of metal, burning and piercing his back.

That first day was very long. The clamshell was burning hot during the day, but as night came on, it cooled, giving some relief until it turned shivering cold. When at last the lid was opened, Harold felt relief and also helplessness. His legs were numb; yet, he had to make them work, if he was to live. He drank his root broth meal and fell to the ground to sleep. Each day, more prisoners came. In a dreadful way, that helped as they had to take turns in the clamshells. Sometimes, each prisoner had a turn to be questioned.

Harold's answers were always the same:

"Harold E. Bellmer, Private, First Class, 1412304." He was slapped many times, and the Germans would ask him over and over about his last name and tried to trick him on the spelling. His answer was always the same, Harold E. Bellmer, B E L L M E R. Harold could not understand why his name was so important to them. Harold stayed DETERMINED to do right, give no information except name, rank, and serial number; and LIVE!

All too soon, it would be his turn in the clamshell again. He lost count of the days and time. His goal was to stay alive and hopefully someday return home to America and that little town in Iowa named Dunkerton.

But he wondered, how much time did he have?

Time is Running Out

Legs are aching,
Back is hurting-
Will these spikes ever stop?
How can I breathe,
Lord, help me to live!
Time of consciousness is running out and gone...

Suddenly the top is lifted!
Hands grab me and pull me up.
I cannot stand, my legs are numb,
But <u>air</u>, sweet <u>air!</u>
I am still alive for this time, till next,
For another moment or day.
THANK YOU, LORD!

Food and drink are the same-
The liquid roots have been boiled in.
Weakness, how long can I keep on-
Time is running out.
Give me strength, Lord!
Life is small, the same, over and over-
There is not time: only existence.

Chapter 17

Harold did not know it, but back in America, and even France and Germany, things were happening. On July 16, 1918, the American Red Cross sent Harold's Father, Charles, a letter giving their sympathy and acknowledging the anxiety he must be feeling. It told him of the procedures taking place to find Harold. The American Red Cross was able to work in France, but the International Red Cross worked in other nations. Germany was very slow in giving out any information and was not letting the Red Cross actively investigate in their country. BUT things were changing in Germany.

They had already forced all the able-bodied men into fighting. That left only the very old and crippled to work the farms and grow the food for their soldiers. Also, the more soldiers they had, the more food they needed. Kaiser Wilhelm II ordered all horses to be collected for the army's use. That left the farmers to work their farms by hand. Food was becoming scarce, and the prisoner population was becoming larger.

The International Red Cross was able to convince Germany that the American Red Cross would be willing to help provide for the American prisoners. There were certain conditions: each prisoner would have to meet with a Red Cross worker and fill out a card, stating his health. Oh, Oh, the clamshells! Thankfully, by now, the Germans needed the help bad enough to remove the clamshells, which were probably turned into bullets. On August 11, 1918, Harold filled out a card that identified him as a prisoner of war in Germany.

In November, Charles and Mabel received an American Red Cross Telegram dated November 15, 1918, saying Harold E. Bellmer was a prisoner in Camp Rastatt, Germany. A copy of the card

Harold had filled out was at the bottom. He had dated it August 11. It took from August to November for Harold's family to find out; **but Harold was alive!**

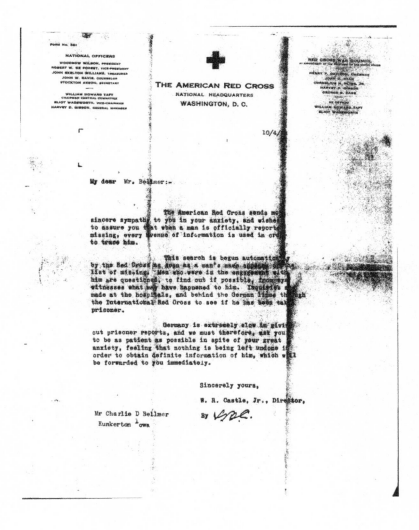

Chapter 18

One day in the fall, German soldiers loaded several prisoners, Harold included, into the back of a truck. They did not know where they were going so this was scary. They always marched the prisoners from place to place, but maybe with the Red Cross intervention there was a new plan.

Are we being taken someplace to be killed? Harold wondered. No one spoke. The prisoners had learned very quickly after capture that talking and asking questions only made the situation much worse. The Germans were very much in charge and accepted no talking.

The truck finally stopped in the little town of Illmensee. When the prisoners climbed out of the truck, they were surprised to see where they were and the crowd that had gathered. The soldiers counted and only let off the amount needed for this town. The old men left in town were each counted out the number of prisoners they had signed up to take. Harold and two others went with a man dressed in farm clothing. He spoke no English, and the prisoners only knew the German commands they had been given and forced to do. Thankfully, an English-speaking soldier gave them a few instructions:

Soldiers would be checking on them and the Germans taking them.

They were to obey their German employer.

They were not to go into the German's house or use any of his personal belongings.

They were to obey the German employer and work well for him or would be taken back to prison camp and punished accordingly.

Papers were signed, and soon, they were walking down a dirt road out into the countryside. Harold looked around. It was nice to see the open area, but, being a farmer, it was sad to see the condition the farms were in. After they had rounded a corner, the farmer stopped, turned to the prisoners and smiled. He put his hand on his chest and said his name. They each repeated it, and he did the same. It was a friendly introduction, but the men still did not know where they were going or what they would be doing for sure, Harold guessed the man was a farmer, but they could be headed to another town, also.

Sooner than Harold expected, the man stopped. He looked at them, then turned and pointed up a long drive. The men could see a house and a barn, both in need of repair. There was a plow left in a field, abandoned. It was a sad sight, and yet it was so encouraging to Harold and the other two men.

Chapter 19

When the four men came walking up the drive, a woman came out of the house. She was old, like her husband but had a big smile of welcome for the American prisoners. She led the men to the well and filled the bucket, then served each of the men a drink. They knew they were among friends and had nothing to fear from these people that were now in charge of them. The man put his hand on his chest and said his name, then took his wife's hand and said her name. Harold quickly introduced himself with a slight bow. The other men quickly followed Harold's example.

Thus, Harold became the leader of their group. He had been a prisoner the longest and had been taught manners back home in Dunkerton. The others naturally followed, partly because they did not know what to do and partly because they were afraid. They were very willing to let Harold take the lead and be the one to get into trouble if he did something wrong. Harold was depending on God to help him to know what to do.

The farmer took the men to the barn and showed them the straw that would be their bed. Then, he took them out to the back steps of the house. There were three bowls of "soup." They were thrilled to find a few potato chunks in this soup. After eating and licking their bowls clean, the farmer came out and took them to the field where the plow was. From his gestures and what he said in German, the men guessed he was telling them about the German soldiers coming and taking his horses, leaving part of the potato harvest still in the ground. The prisoners could tell he was upset.

Harold picked up one horse's side of the double harness and put it over his head. He indicated for one of the others to do likewise.

The other two frowned, but Harold said quietly, "Do you want to live or die? Remember, our job is to stay alive and one day go home."

One of the others followed Harold's example.

The farmer smiled and nodded his head, "Yes;" then he lifted the harness off each of the men. Leading them back to the barn, he turned to face them, gave a nod of his head, and said, "*Gute Nacht*," then pointed to the men.

They all repeated, "*Gute Nacht*." The farmer shook his head with a frown; then, he pointed to the men.

Harold thought his eyes almost looked pleading, so Harold said hesitantly in English, "Good night."

The farmer's face lit up as he struggled to say it. "Goot Nite." He turned and walked to the house.

The three men turned and went into the barn. The one that always hung back now tried to take the lead. He wanted to leave and make a run for freedom.

At first, the other prisoner seemed to go along, but Harold asked, "Where will you go? Do you know which way is North or South? Where are the German soldiers? How will you avoid them? Remember, if they see you, you will be shot—no questions asked. This farmer not only needs help, but he WANTS to HELP US! Don't throw away an opportunity to live."

With that, Harold burrowed into the straw and went to sleep.

Chapter 20

After the best sleep the three prisoners had in a long time, they woke refreshed, encouraged. In a way, to say why, was hard. They were still prisoners, and the German soldiers could show up at any time. Now, it wasn't just them that would be checked on; it would also be the farmer and his wife. The encouraging thing was that they were out of the prison camp and on a farm.

Harold had an advantage over the other two men. He had been raised on a farm, so he knew the work. He had also helped his father build houses, and Harold noticed right away, many repairs were needed on the buildings.

While they ate the thin, gruel breakfast, Harold tried to talk to the farmer. After much gesturing and repeating of words, both in English and German, they were beginning to figure out what each other were saying.

The farmer's face lit up when he realized Harold was a farmer. It was a relief to the other prisoners to know that Harold understood the work. They were disappointed when they found out they would be doing it WITH Harold but soon realized how helpful Harold was.

The four men set out for the field. Harold showed the other two prisoners how to hold the plow, so it would dig in and turn up the soil. Then, he told one to come with him and went to the front where the harness had been left on the ground. Harold picked up and put the harness over his head, settling it on his shoulders. The other man just looked at him, with a scowl.

Harold instructed him to harness up as he had, saying, "Remember we're here to work and to LIVE, so we can go back home when this is over." The man put the harness on as Harold had. Harold then showed him how to lean into the harness and pull. Throughout the day, the three prisoners took turns pulling the plow. The farmer and part of the time his wife also picked up the potatoes. The farmer and his wife kept smiling as they worked. To have help was good.

Suddenly, the plowing stopped as one of the men sneezed, "Ah-Ah-AHCHOO!" Sleeping in the hay was causing a reaction.

"Gesundheit." replied the farmer and his wife in unison. Everyone looked at each other and smiled. It was a moment that brought them all close together in the awful reality of war.

By supper time, they were able to look back and see what they had accomplished. Not as much as horses could have, but the farmer was pleased. While they sat outside and ate their potato soup supper, Harold, through words, pointing, and actions, told the farmer that he could see places the house and barn needed to be fixed. The farmer was surprised and glad to find out that Harold knew how to fix things but explained that he had no nails.

They were beginning to form a way of communicating and understanding each other.

After supper, while the other men rested, Harold and the farmer walked around and looked at things. In the end, the farmer found nails that could be pulled, straightened, and reused. The next day, Harold worked on the nails and buildings, being careful not to "fix" too much. They did not want to upset the soldiers. If any came by, Harold would hurry to the field, sometimes fastening his pants, as if he had been to the outhouse.

Each Sunday, the men would walk to town and pick up a Red Cross package. This was part of the bargain that was made with Germany: the American Red Cross would provide food for the American prisoners. This allowed them to talk a little with other prisoners. Harold and the other two men soon realized how good they had it. Not everyone was kind and friendly. Harold silently praised God for how He helped and protected him.

Chapter 21

The three prisoners began counting the time and weeks by Sunday, as that was the day to go to town and meet the Red Cross truck. It became almost a holiday for the prisoners and the farmers. Harold, loving to laugh, would often do something along the way to get the others to laugh.

On this trip, suddenly one of the prisoners sneezed. Just as the farmer started to say, "*Gesundheit*," Harold let out a big sneeze and nudged the third prisoner, who then let out a big sneeze. The farmer ended up saying, "*Gesundheit, Gesundheit, Gesundheit*!!!" It made the farmer sound like he was sneezing, and they all had to stop walking, they were laughing so hard.

Sadness always came when someone was missing, because that could only mean that they had not survived the week. Times were hard, and many German farmers took their frustration out on the prisoners they were in charge of. Harold had helped his two prison mates to understand that, as tough as things got, be determined to LIVE and RETURN HOME. They had been able to help their farmer, which, in turn, helped them. They even shared some of the Red Cross supplies with the farmer and his wife. No one ate big meals, but the wife was a good cook, and they had better meals by sharing.

On one particular Sunday, Harold and the other prisoners had a pleasant surprise. They were given paper and pencils and allowed to write a letter.

Harold wrote:

November 3, 1918

Dear Loving Father,
I am well and feeLing fine and hope you all are the same. I am getting an Red Cross box each weak. Every Sunday I have to come to this little town of Illmensel and here is where I get my boxes. This

weak I got a pair of pantes and a pair of socks and a sut of wooles under wear. All is American goods. In the box is 12 boxes of hard bread, 2 cans of roast beef, 2 cans of corn beef, 1 salmon, 1sweet corn, 1 tomatoes, 2 cans of peas, 5 sacks of smoking tobacco, and 5 folders of cigarette papers. I am out hear on a farm they treat me good. Tell Myrtle Hello for me and that I am well and cuming home some day when the woar is ended. Well I will have to close for this time. My address is on the other side. I will make a line whear it is. Well I will close, I am Your Loving Sun Harold

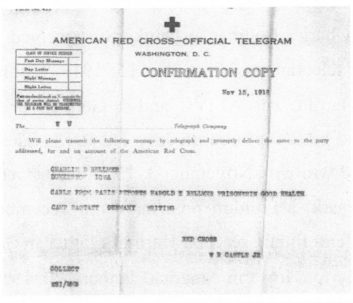

Charles Bellmer in Dunkerton received a Red Cross telegram on November 15, 1918, telling him that Harold was ALIVE and a German prisoner. He had been captured on July 16, 1918. The letter Harold wrote on November 3, 1918, had a German post mark, a London post mark on December 31, 1918, and finally reached Harold's father in Dunkerton, Iowa in America. January 20, 1919.

(Author's Note: Please do not judge Harold on his spelling. Remember, he only had 8 years of schooling, and most of that time, he had no mother, so he did the farm chores, more than schoolwork.

Also in 1918, the cancer-causing effects of cigarette smoking were not known. Sadly, Harold and most soldiers of that time suffered with CANCER later in life.)

Chapter 22

November 10, 1918, went as normal for Harold, the other two prisoners, and the farmer. They walked to Illmensel for the Red Cross delivery. Harold hoped his letter had reached home and that he might have a return letter. He had no way of knowing how long it would take.

Harold worked hard to keep his spirits up, but with little to no information, he wondered sometimes if he would ever get home. Again, this week, there were a couple of prisoners they did not see. That was sad for all the prisoners; it meant they were too sick to come or had not made it through the week. The Red Cross workers always joked and tried to cheer the prisoners up but were not allowed to give out much information about the war. They had to be neutral in order to remain in Germany and help the prisoners.

The farmers in the area did have a communication system that reminded Harold of the Prayer Chain back home. When someone heard some update or important news about a family member or the war, the news would go from house to house. It had to go carefully, since German soldiers could come past at any time. Often, the women would go, taking trails through the woods, always with a basket for collecting herbs and edible plants along the way. They were less likely to see a soldier, and if they did, they were just out collecting food. At times, they would give the soldiers some of the herbs to nibble on as they went on their way.

Monday, November 11, 1918, was a normal day for Harold and his fellow prisoners. They were out in the new clothes they had received the day before. Since it was fall, they were thankful for the added warmth. As they were working, one of the men noticed a neighbor lady hurrying to the house.

The farmer was in with his wife at the time.

All of a sudden, the farmer came running out to the field yelling, "DOWN WITH KAISER! DOWN WITH KAISER!" The prisoners stopped and stared at the farmer as he came. Harold was thankful the farmer had wanted them to teach him English words, and they were thankful to hear it in English. There was no mistake about what he was saying. THE WAR WAS OVER!

Chapter 23

December 18, 1918, Charles D. Bellmer, in Dunkerton, Iowa, received a telegram sent from Washington:

Your Son Private Harold E. Bellmer officially reported releases from German Prison Camp at Rastatt. Returned to France in good health.

Harris _____, General

What rejoicing there was in Dunkerton, Iowa, that day as the message of Harold being safe in France was told and retold throughout the town!

The war was over on November 11, 1918, but for Harold and the other prisoners in Germany, they were still a long way from HOME. The farmer went to town to see what he could find out. No one knew when or how the prisoners would get home.

Eventually, the word came for all the prisoners to be in Illmensel at a specified time. Saying "Good-bye" to the farmer and his wife was sad and happy at the same time. They had been good to Harold and the other two prisoners while on their farm. Having them had been a help to the elderly couple, also. Harold prayed that they would have family members returning from the war to help them. They said their "Good-byes" on the farm. The wife cried and wished them well. She remained at the farm while her husband walked with them into town. It was a quiet walk; that is, until Harold said a loud, "Ah-choo"!

The other two Prisoners quickly followed with "Ah-choo"! "Ah-choo"! The farmer said, *"Gesundheit! Gesundheit! Gesundheit!"* and they all had one good, last laugh together.

In town, the prisoners were quickly being loaded onto trucks by the German soldiers. They were not happy that the war had been lost so were of mixed emotion. They would be a little rough at times, but they were also eager to get home to their own families, so hurried everyone along. The sooner they got this war mess cleaned up, the sooner they could go home, also. Harold and the others did not know where they were going but soon found out they were going to Rastatt: the same camp where they started and the clamshell tortures had been. When they arrived, they were glad to see the empty field. They were held there until all the prisoners for both sides were accounted for, and an "exchange" was arranged. They were treated better than before but had to answer questions and fill out paperwork. Thankfully, the American Red Cross was there, also.

Harold was thankful to be in France before Christmas, but he was still a long way from home. HOME! How long would it take to get there? Harold still had a long way to go. March 22, 1919, on the ship *Siboney*, Harold left St. Nazaire, France. While on the ship, Harold caught the MUMPS and was put in the infirmary isolation ward with the others on the ship that were sick. Upon reaching Ellis Island in the New York harbor, Harold was transported to the hospital. Upon recovery, Harold was sent to Fort Dodge, Iowa. This was a much more comfortable ride than his last train ride in France. Finally, in April of 1919, at Fort Dodge, Iowa, Harold was mustered out of the army and on his way HOME!

Harold Bellmer
in the U.S., Army Transport Service, Passenger Lists, 1910-1939

Name:	Harold Bellmer
Departure Date:	22 Mar 1919 {1919}
Departure Place:	St Nazaire, France
Arrival Date:	1918-1919
Address:	R.F.D. 2
Residence Place:	Dunkerton, Iowa
Father:	Charley O. Bellmer
Ship:	SIBONEY
Military Unit:	364TH INF.
Rank:	Private
Service Number:	1, 412, 304
Roles:	COMPANY K, 364TH INFANTRY
Search Photos:	Search for 'SIBONEY' in the US WWI Troop Transport Ship Photos collection

Source Citation

The National Archives at College Park, College Park, Maryland; Record Group Title: Records of the Office of the Quartermaster General, 1774-1985; Record Group Number: 92; Roll or Box Number: 169

Source Information

Ancestry.com. U.S., Army Transport Service, Passenger Lists, 1910-1939 [database on-line]. Lehi, UT, USA: Ancestry.com Operations, Inc., 2016.

Original data:

Lists of Incoming Passengers, 1917-1938. Textual records: 360 Boxes: 948 [NAI ID]. Records of the Office of the Quartermaster General, 1774-1985, Record Group 92. The National Archives at College Park, Maryland.
Lists of Outgoing Passengers, 1917-1938. Textual records: 105 Boxes: 948 [NAI ID]. Records of the Office of the Quartermaster General, 1774-1985, Record Group 92. The National Archives at College Park, Maryland.

Description

This collection consists of lists of passengers arriving at U.S. ports on Army ships. In addition to troops, passengers could also include nurses and other support personnel, family members, and any other passengers who may have been traveling onboard these ships. In some instances, troops from other countries traveled on U.S. Army ships as well. Learn more...

© 2021, Ancestry.com

U.S., WWI Troop Transport Ships, 1918-1919

Photo # NH 103238-A   USS Siboney in New York Harbor

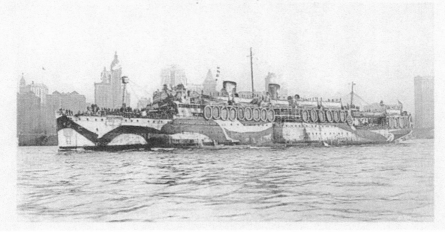

97

Chapter 24

What a joyous reunion it was when Harold reached home! Since he had not been able to notify his family, he just showed up. The first in town to see him happened to be his friend Walt. The lumber yard where Walt worked was not far from the tracks. He knew from the uniform and duffel bag, it had to be Harold. Walt gave a yell and ran to embrace his friend. Others in town heard and came running. Thankfully, someone raced on horseback out to his father's farm and told his family.

While Charles went to bring his son home, Mabel started cooking. She wanted a good meal ready for the family as soon as possible. Roland, Lee, and Ivan were waiting at the end of the drive, each trying to see the wagon coming before the others. As they turned the corner on their road, all three started jumping up and down, yelling and waving at the same time.

After hugs and a little tickling from Harold for his brothers, they went into the house. Mabel quickly moved things off the hot parts of the stove and gathered Harold into her arms. How thin he seemed! She felt like he was skin and bones, but she didn't say anything.

Mabel just thought, *"Give me a little time and I'll soon have some meat on those bones!*

All evening, friends from town stopped by to welcome Harold home. Some brought gifts of food, and everyone told Harold they had been praying for him. He was very thankful, and by the time the last left, he was exhausted. How good his own bed felt! His father and Mabel kept everyone quiet the next morning and let Harold sleep. It was almost time for lunch when he finally woke up! He received a lot of good-natured teasing about that, but everyone was as glad to have him home as Harold was to BE HOME!

Chapter 25

Harold quickly settled into the farm work. To have all the equipment needed and the whole family working together was wonderful. In the afternoon, Mabel saw Harold lift the lid on the catfish tank that he and his father had put in so many years ago.

"There are some good-sized fish in there," Mabel said. "How about catfish for supper?"

"Sounds delicious!" Harold answered. "Can the boys help me catch some?"

"It's fine with me if it is ok with your father." Mabel smiled and thought, *I better put some towels by the door, they will probably come in all wet.*

Supper was delicious, and Mabel was right: the towels were needed for four happy boys.

Church on Sunday was full. Everyone in town had heard that Harold was home, and the minister had sent out the word for a potluck lunch after the morning service.

Harold's shoulder was sore from all the welcome slaps on the back, but they were nothing compared to the clamshells the Germans used. He had not mentioned that to anyone yet, but he had told his father about the farming conditions over there.

During the day, Walt's Dad asked what the German countryside was like? Harold told about the huge trees in the forest and how the farmer's wife would go to the woods to find herbs and things they could eat.

The conversation ended with Mr. Miller saying, "That's where you're from, you know. In fact, that's where most of us are from." Many people said a quiet yes or nodded their heads, indicating their families were from Germany. Harold silently decided he needed to talk to his father when they got home.

Erma and Elsie were busy helping the women by playing games with the younger children. Elsie noticed Erma look over at Harold several times and mentioned it to her. Erma replied simply, "I'm so glad and thankful he is home safe."

That night after the milking and the younger boys went to bed, Harold asked his father about being German. "Yes," Charles answered. "My father and mother, John and Elen Belmar came from Germany."

"I did not know," Harold replied quietly. "The Germans kept asking me about my last name. I could not figure out why it mattered so much to them."

"When John and Elen came from Germany, it was spelled BELMAR. Then, in 1900, the Census taker said it was spelled BELLMAR, and in 1905, the Iowa Census taker spelled it BELLMER. We, being Americans, just changed the spelling each time they did. After all, we speak English, so we spell our name the English way."

"Thank you for doing that, Father." Harold answered. "I did not know, thankfully. The German guards treated the American prisoners of German descent as traitors. They had it much worse than I did. Now I know why they questioned me so much about my name. I am thankful I did not know then. I could honestly tell them my name is Bellmer, B E L L M E R."

Chapter 26

The four friends from school days began to renew their friendship by doing things together. As summer came on and the crops were planted, they would go with Erma's Father, Mr. Goff, and help him with the tent revivals. Sometimes, it was helping with harvests, going from farm to farm to help as needed. Harold often went with his father, at first, then by himself, to help build houses. Harold found he really enjoyed house building, and he was good at it. This became his life's work. He loved to fix broken things, and when a load needed to be taken to the dump, he would volunteer. After emptying the load, he would walk around and find things that he could fix--a table with a broken leg to him was an easy fix.

One day, Walt asked Harold a special question. "Harold, you're my best friend. Would you stand up with me when Elsie and I get married?"

"You asked her, and she said yes to YOU?" Harold teased. "Of course, I will. When is the wedding? Do you have a place to live yet? How about furniture? I fixed a table last night. Now all I need is some chairs, and you have a dining room!" Harold laughed.

On January 7, 1920, Walt and Elsie became Mr. and Mrs. Walt Baer, with Harold and Erma standing beside them.

One year after the World War I ended, on November 11,1920, Elsie and Walt did the same for Harold and Erma, as they became Mr. and Mrs. Harold Bellmer. The two couples lived all their lives in Dunkerton, Iowa, having homes one street apart. They remained lifelong friends.

Harold and Erma had four children, eighteen grandchildren, and innumerable great and great-

great grandchildren. Every generation has had members that proudly served in the military, so we at home in America can live FREE!

Harold and Erma Bellmar in their wedding picture,
November 11, 1920

This how I remember Grandpa and Grandma, happy and loving to laugh!

THE EVENING COURIER AND REPOR

WAS A PRISONER IN GERMAN CAMP

Addendum

As reported in The Waterloo *Evening Courier*, May 13,1919, page 7, there was an interview and report of Harold's POW experience. The reporter stated that he was the only POW from that part of Iowa. He also asked Harold if he experienced or knew of any of the extreme cruelties said to have been inflicted on prisoners by the Germans. Knowing Grandpa (Harold) as I did, I can only guess as to why he denied what he endured. Grandpa loved to laugh and have fun. He probably was still healing both physically and emotionally from what he had endured. Why talk about the bad and have to relive it? He was home in America and safe. That's what mattered. He did the job that needed done, but now he was home, safe.

In the early 1960s, I had a history report to do for homework. My mother suggested that I ask my grandpa if I could interview him for the report. Surprisingly, he did allow it. I will never forget him lifting the back of his shirt and T-shirt. Remembering the sight of those rows of scars from the clamshell spikes brings tears to my eyes even now.

October 17,1971, Harold Bellmer went to Heaven, having asked Jesus Christ to forgive and save him as a young teen when he helped Olin Goff with the tent revivals. Since his passing, I have talked with my siblings and cousins; none of them knew that Grandpa was a POW. Everyone knew he served in the military in WWI. I am thankful for my mother suggesting I ask Grandpa and that enough time had passed that he told me about what he experienced, so *I can live free!*

I would like to once again say,

THANK YOU!

To all our VETERANS and MILITARY!

About the Author

Florenda Burns taught Kindergarten for 25 years and also served children at The Children's Center Rehabilitation Hospital for 16 years.

She has written Sunday School curriculum for two-and-three-year-olds. She lives in Yukon, Oklahoma with her family and her Service Dog, Oreo.

Picture and Document Placement

As you view these documents, you will notice dates and events do not always seen to match. Please remember the mail system was not as fast as today, it was wartime and not all mail could go straight through. Some things have postmarks from three different countries.

1. Harold in uniform, sitting in fancy chair: COVER
2. Registration Card: Chapter 9
3. Windsor Castle Letter: Before Chapter 13
4. Picture of *Runic*: Chapter 13,
5. Picture of Harold in France: Chapter 13
6. Prisoner Identification, End of Chapter 15
7. Red Cross Letter 10/4/1918: Chapter17
8. *Kriegsgefangenensendung* Oct 29 (International Red Cross Postcard to Mr Chas D. Bellmer, has 3 postmarks.} The back {second page} Reply to: Name Harold Bellmer Prisoner Nr. 80738: Beginning of Chapter 18
9. Harold wrote to his Father 11/3/1918 Chapter 21
10. American Red Cross Telegram 11/15/1918

11. Telegram received at 8:14 am, 12/18/1918 Beginning of Chapter 23

12. Transport service passenger list for Harold and Picture of USS *Siboney*, End of Chapter 23

13. Wedding Picture of Harold and Erma Bellmer, After Chapter 26

14. Picture of my laughing Grandpa Harold and happy Grandma Erma Bellmer, After Chapter 26

15. Newspaper article, WAS A PRISONER IN GERMAN CAMP, Next to Addendum